W9-BNT-636

41858074R00057

Made in the USA
Middletown, DE
24 March 2017

THE NEW AMERICAN HAGGADAH

Ken Royal and Lauren Royal

Novelty Books

THE NEW AMERICAN HAGGADAH by Ken Royal and Lauren Royal

Published by Novelty Books, a division of Novelty Publishers, LLC, 205 Avenida Del Mar #275, San Clemente, CA 92674

4th Edition, February 2017

Cover by Brent Royal-Gordon

Book Design by Jack Royal-Gordon

ISBN 978-1-938907-99-9

Dedicated to our family...
past, present and future

PREFACE

This is the fourth edition of the New American *Haggadah*. Our purpose in creating this version was to blend the traditions of the Passover Seder with modern American Jewish culture.

The history of Judaism is replete with rebirths and renewals of ceremonial traditions. Part of the spirit of Judaism is the constant reformation of traditions. Since the Exodus from Egypt, which occurred from about 1280 to 1270 BCE, there have been over 3000 different *Haggadot* in many languages. Although the core is always the same, the story is often retold from different points of view, in keeping with the notion that "in every generation, everyone must think of himself or herself as having personally left Egypt." Therefore, each generation must carry the torch, but in their own way. This *Haggadah* represents our way.

Our *Haggadah* focuses on the positive aspects of our customs, particularly freedom and tolerance. It communicates these values using traditional Hebrew songs and prayers with supporting *Torah* text, but explains ideas and history in modern English so that we can understand and appreciate them. Although it is new and American, it is based on the *Seders* of our ancestors, and continues the traditions, prayers, songs, words, and rituals of our past so that our family and others can truly share and appreciate our heritage.

Ken Royal and Lauren Royal
March 2012

ITEMS NEEDED FOR *SEDER*
(besides place settings, wine, and dinner)

Two candlesticks with candles for candle lighting

Matches or lighter for candle lighting

Pitcher, bowl, and towels for the first washing of the hands

Pre-moistened hand towels (ready to quickly heat in the microwave) for the second washing of the hands

Elijah's Cup

Plate with three *matzot* (covered)

Napkin or bag to cover *afikoman*

Main *Seder* plate: horseradish, roasted lamb shank, roasted egg, scoop of *charoset,* parsley, romaine lettuce, and a small orange

Individual *Seder* plates: each with a *matzah* broken into four pieces, a mini bowl of saltwater, two or more thin slices of horseradish root, a sprig of parsley, a scoop of *charoset*, and a peeled hard-boiled egg

CHAROSET RECIPE

Serves about 20

- 9 apples, peeled, cored, and shredded in food processor
- 16 ounces finely chopped ("baking size") pecans
- 2 tablespoons sugar
- grated rind of 2 lemons
- sweet red wine to taste (anything from a few tablespoons to half a bottle)

Put shredded apples in a strainer and press well to remove extra moisture. Combine in mixing bowl with other ingredients. Refrigerate until served.

INSTRUCTIONS

One person is designated as the leader of the *Seder*. The leader begins the ceremony, as indicated by the parenthetical statement: "The leader says."

Much of the service is recited by one participant at a time, moving counter-clockwise around the gathering when indicated by the words: "Next participant." The leader does not read any of the "Next participant" sections.

The words "All together" signify that everyone, including the leader, should participate.

The statements in bold are recited, including the Hebrew words in italics.

The capitalized parenthetical statements indicate specific behaviors for those attending the *Seder*.

Everyone should pay attention, out of respect for the *Seder*, and so they know when it is their turn!

THE *SEDER*

(EVERYONE TAKES THEIR PLACE AROUND THE TABLE AND FILLS THEIR CUP WITH WINE BEFORE BEGINNING.)

(The leader says):
Among the ceremonies that sustain our Jewish heritage, especially beloved is the *Seder*, celebrated on Passover Eve, which is also called *Pesach*. The name *Seder* means "order," as in the order of the service. By reading the words of this *Haggadah* and by eating symbolic foods, we obey the *mitzvah* written in the *Torah*: "You shall tell the *Pesach* story to your children in the days to come." The story we tell is how the Jewish people were freed from being slaves in Egypt. We call this the Exodus.

The first ritual is the candle lighting, which is traditionally performed by the females in the home. Ladies, please rise, gather around the candles, and perform the lighting ceremony.

(THE FEMALES GATHER AROUND THE
CANDLES, LIGHT THEM, AND TOGETHER
RECITE THE FOLLOWING BLESSINGS.)

בָּרוּךְ אַתָּה אֲדֹנָי אֱלֹהֵינוּ מֶלֶךְ הָעוֹלָם, אֲשֶׁר קִדְּשָׁנוּ
בְּמִצְוֹתָיו וְצִוָּנוּ לְהַדְלִיק נֵר שֶׁל יוֹם טוֹב.

*Baruch atah Adonai Ellohaynu mellach
ha'olam asher kid'shanu b'mitzvasov v'tzivanu
l'hadlik nair shel yom tov.*

Blessed art Thou, Eternal our God, King of
the Universe, who has sanctified us by Thy
commandments, and has commanded us to
kindle the festival lights.

בָּרוּךְ אַתָּה אֲדֹנָי אֱלֹהֵינוּ מֶלֶךְ הָעוֹלָם, שֶׁהֶחֱיָנוּ
וְקִיְּמָנוּ וְהִגִּיעָנוּ לַזְּמַן הַזֶּה.

*Baruch atah Adonai Ellohaynu mellach
ha'olam shehecheyanu v'kiy'manu v'higianu
lazman hazzeh.*

Blessed art Thou, Eternal our God, King of
the Universe, who has kept us alive and well
so that we can celebrate this special time.

May our home be consecrated, O God, by the
light of Thy countenance, shining upon us in
blessing, and bringing us peace!

8

(All together):
May the candles remind us that we must help and not hurt, cause joy and not sorrow, create and not destroy, and help all to be free. We praise God for the gift of life and this happy time.

(The leader says):
Everyone please be seated. It is now time for us to raise our first cup of wine.

(THE FEMALES TAKE THEIR SEATS. EVERYONE PICKS UP THE FIRST CUP OF WINE.)

(The leader says):
In the *Pesach* story we are told four times, in different ways, that God promised freedom to our people. We remember each of these promises with a cup of wine. With the first cup of wine we recall the first promise found in the *Torah*: "I am God, and I will free you from the slavery of Egypt."

(All together):

בָּרוּךְ אַתָּה אֲדֹנָי אֱלֹהֵינוּ מֶלֶךְ הָעוֹלָם, בּוֹרֵא פְּרִי
הַגָּפֶן.

Baruch atah Adonai Ellohaynu mellach ha'olam bowray paree hagafen.
Blessed art Thou, Eternal our God, King of the Universe, Creator of the fruit of the vine.

(Next participant):
Blessed art Thou, Eternal our God, King of the Universe, Who has made us holy through Your *mitzvot* and lovingly given us festivals for gladness.

(Next participant):
With love You have given us this Festival of *Matzot*—a celebration of our freedom and a holy time to recall our going out of Egypt.

(All together):
Blessed art Thou, Eternal our God, King of the Universe, Who has given us life and sustenance and brought us to this happy season.

(The leader says):
Let's all drink our first cup of wine.

(EVERYONE DRINKS THE FIRST CUP OF WINE.)

(The leader says):
The next ritual is the washing of the hands. We traditionally wash our hands by taking the pitcher of water in one hand, making a loose fist of the other hand and pouring three small splashes into it, then reversing hands and repeating. Another traditional option is to have one person pour water for everyone else, using the same method. We are not ready to eat our meal yet, so no blessing is recited. After washing your hands, please be seated.

(EVERYONE PROCEEDS TO THE PITCHER AND BOWL AND WASHES THEIR HANDS IN THE TRADITIONAL MANNER. NO BLESSING IS RECITED. AFTER DRYING THEIR HANDS, ALL ARE SEATED.)

(Next participant):
Haggadah means "the telling." As the *Torah* says: "And you shall tell it to your children..." The first formal *Haggadah* was written over two thousand years ago. Over time, prayers, hymns, and selections from the *Mishnah* were added. By the Middle Ages, it was recorded as an addition to the prayerbook. In the thirteenth century it became a separate handwritten book.

(Next participant):
The *Torah* tells us that *Pesach* was the first festival that the Jewish people celebrated more than three thousand years ago. Like us, they gathered together in great joy to celebrate the Exodus. The special meal for *Pesach* is called the *Seder*. The word *Seder* means "order." There is a set order for all the things we do during our *Seder*—things that remind us of the Exodus from Egypt.

(Next participant):
The *Seder* is a joyful blend of influences which have contributed toward inspiring our people, though scattered throughout the world, with a genuine feeling of kinship. Year after year, the *Seder* has thrilled us with an appreciation of the glories of our past, helped us to endure the severest persecutions, and created within us an enthusiasm for the high ideals of freedom. It has helped to forge strong links between individuals and the Jewish people.

(Next participant):
The moral and spiritual worth of the *Seder*, which has become a vital part of the Jewish consciousness, is priceless. We should suffer a horrible loss were the *Seder* allowed to pass into neglect. Averting this danger is the reason we are gathered here tonight.

(THE LEADER POINTS TO THE *SEDER* PLATE and says):
Rabban Gamliel said that whoever does not explain the symbols of the *Seder* has not fulfilled his duty. Therefore, on this special night, it is traditional for the symbols to be explained. On the *Seder* plate the following symbolic foods are found...

(Next participant):

Maror (מָרוֹר), a bitter herb such as the horseradish root, reminds us of the bitterness of slavery in Egypt. As it is written in the *Torah*: "They embittered their lives with hard labor, with mortar and bricks, with every kind of work in the field; all the work which they made them do was rigorous."

(Next participant):

Z'roa (זְרוֹעַ), a roasted lamb shank, reminds us that during the tenth plague the Jews smeared lamb's blood on their doorposts so God would "pass over" their homes and spare their firstborn. This is why this festival is called *Pesach*—or Passover. The roasted lamb shank also reminds us of the special lamb that was brought to the Temple in Jerusalem on *Pesach* as an offering to God.

(Next participant):

Beitsa (בֵּיצָה), a roasted egg. In ancient days on the Jewish festivals of *Pesach*, *Shavuot* and *Sukkot*, our ancestors would bring an offering to the Temple to be roasted in honor of the holiday. The roasted egg reminds us of that sacrifice. The egg is also a symbol of renewal that proclaims hope for future redemption.

(Next participant):

Charoset (חֲרוֹסֶת), a mixture of nuts, apples, sugar, and wine, reminds us of the mortar used in the great structures built by the Jewish slaves for the Pharaoh in Egypt. Not everyone makes *charoset* the same way. *Sephardim* use dates, figs, and nuts. Some Israelis add bananas, but everyone uses red wine to give it a bricklike color.

(Next participant):

Karpas (כַּרְפַּס), a green vegetable such as parsley, reminds us that *Pesach* occurs during the spring, when new life brings a feeling of hope. It is a token of gratitude to God for the products of the earth.

(Next participant):

Hazeret (חֲזֶרֶת), romaine lettuce, is on the *Seder* plate because it tastes sweet at first but then turns bitter. The *Jerusalem Talmud* compares this to the fact that the Egyptians were kind to the Israelites at first, but later embittered their lives.

(Next participant):

 Some families have adopted the custom of placing an orange on the *Seder* plate. This originated from an incident that occurred when women were just beginning to become rabbis. Susannah Heschel spoke about the emerging equality of women in Jewish life. After her talk, an irate man rose and shouted, "A woman belongs on the *bimah* like an orange belongs on the *Seder* plate!" By placing an orange on the *Seder* plate, we assert that women belong wherever Jews carry on a sacred life.

(The leader says):

There are several other traditional elements of *Pesach* that are not on the *Seder* plate but have important meaning.

(Next participant):

Mei melach (מֵי מֶלַח), the saltwater, reminds us of the sad and bitter tears shed by our people when they were slaves, as well as the tears of those not free today. We will dip the *karpas* in the saltwater.

(Next participant):

Yayin (יַיִן) is the wine that we drink. At the *Seder*, as in other Jewish ceremonies, such as the Sabbath, marriages, *Bar Mitzvahs*, and the naming of a child, wine is used as a token of festivity.

(Next participant):

The four cups of wine that we drink during the meal remind us of God's four promises of freedom for the Jewish people: "I will bring you out...I will deliver you...I will redeem you...I will take you to be my people."

(Next participant):

The Cup of Elijah is filled with wine and set aside in hopes that the prophet Elijah will visit us during the *Seder*. The rabbis of long ago taught that Elijah will come and announce a time when all people will be free.

(Next participant):

Matzah (מַצָּה) is perhaps the most recognizable and important symbol of Passover. We eat *matzah* to remind us of how our ancestors had to leave Egypt in such haste that the dough for their bread did not have time to rise. *Matzah* has holes to keep it from rising. Passover *matzah* is carefully watched from the time the wheat is cut until the *matzah* is finally baked, so that no moisture causes it to become leavened.

(Next participant):

To make *matzah*, the dough must be worked for no longer than eighteen minutes, or the natural process of fermentation, or leavening, will occur. *Matzah* is a metaphor for our own lives. It teaches us that if we want to achieve freedom, we cannot just sit back and let nature take its course.

(Next participant):

Matzah is both the bread of slavery and the bread of freedom. It is the only Passover symbol with two opposing meanings. The three *matzot* on the table remind us there are three kinds of people: those who are not yet free, those who are free but don't care about the freedom of others, and those who are free and work to help others become free.

(The leader says):
We now each take a sprig of parsley and hold it up.

(EVERYONE TAKES A SPRIG OF PARSLEY AND HOLDS IT UP.)

(The leader says):
It is time for our first ritual of eating. As we say a blessing and eat a green herb, we remember that it was springtime when the *Pesach* story took place. We dip the greens in saltwater to remind us of the tears of our ancestors who suffered cruel slavery. Please dip your parsley now.

(EVERYONE DIPS THEIR PARSLEY INTO SALTWATER.)

(All together):
בָּרוּךְ אַתָּה אֲדֹנָי אֱלֹהֵינוּ מֶלֶךְ הָעוֹלָם, בּוֹרֵא פְּרִי הָאֲדָמָה.

Baruch atah Adonai Ellohaynu mellach ha'olam bowray paree ha'adamah.

Blessed art Thou, Eternal our God, King of the Universe, Creator of the fruit of the earth.

(The leader says):
Let's all eat our parsley.

(EVERYONE EATS THEIR PARSLEY.)

(The leader says):
It's now time to uncover the *matzah* plate.

(THE LEADER UNCOVERS THE *MATZAH* PLATE FOR ALL TO SEE.)

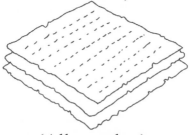

(All together):
This is the bread of affliction our forefathers ate in the land of Egypt. All who are hungry—let them come and eat. All who are needy—let them come and celebrate the Passover with us. May God redeem us from all trouble and from all servitude. Next year at this season, may the whole house of Israel be free!

(The leader continues):
I will now break the middle *matzah* and put half aside until after the meal, for the *afikoman*.

(THE LEADER BREAKS THE MIDDLE
MATZAH, LEAVES HALF OF IT ON THE
PLATE, THEN WRAPS THE OTHER HALF
IN A NAPKIN OR *AFIKOMAN* BAG AND
SETS IT ASIDE.)

(Next participant):
No blessing is said when we break the middle
matzah, since it is broken as a symbol of
incompleteness. It reminds us of *tikkun*
(תִּקּוּן)—all that needs repair in our world. As
we celebrate here, we think of Jews
everywhere. This year all Jews are not yet
fully free. Let all share with us *Pesach's* hope
for freedom: Next year all shall be fully free.

(Next participant):
After the meal, we will all share the *afikoman*.
Again, there will be no blessing. This will
affirm our belief that completeness will come
in the future. Sharing *afikoman* reminds us
that long ago the special gifts brought to the
Temple in Jerusalem were shared. No matter
where people live, sharing bread is a way of
saying, "You are my friend."

(The leader says):
While I cover the *matzah*, please fill your cups
for the second cup of wine.

21

(THE LEADER COVERS THE *MATZAH* PLATE. EVERYONE FILLS THEIR CUP FOR THE SECOND CUP OF WINE.)

(The leader says):
The *Maggid* section of the *Haggadah*, which tells the story of Passover, begins with The Four Questions. In the original *Haggadah* text, one of The Four Questions referred to the Passover Sacrifice. Since the destruction of the Temple in Jerusalem, we do not offer sacrifices, so a question about reclining while eating was substituted. It is traditional for the children to ask The Four Questions in song.

(The children sing an introductory question):
מַה נִּשְׁתַּנָּה הַלַּיְלָה הַזֶּה
מִכָּל הַלֵּילוֹת, מִכָּל הַלֵּילוֹת
הַלַּיְלָה הַזֶּה, הַלַּיְלָה הַזֶּה, מִכָּל הַלֵּילוֹת
הַלַּיְלָה הַזֶּה, הַלַּיְלָה הַזֶּה, מִכָּל הַלֵּילוֹת

Mah nishtanah halailah hazeh
mikol haleilot, mikol halelilot
Halailah hazeh, halailah hazeh, mikol haleilot
Halailah hazeh, halailah hazeh, mikol haleilot

Why is this night different from all other nights?

(The adults answer):

This night is different from all other nights to remind us that the Jewish people were once slaves in Egypt. God, with great strength, helped us go free.

(The children sing the First Question):

שֶׁבְּכָל הַלֵּילוֹת אָנוּ אוֹכְלִין
חָמֵץ וּמַצָּה, חָמֵץ וּמַצָּה
הַלַּיְלָה הַזֶּה, הַלַּיְלָה הַזֶּה כֻּלּוֹ מַצָּה
הַלַּיְלָה הַזֶּה, הַלַּיְלָה הַזֶּה כֻּלּוֹ מַצָּה

Sheb'chol haleilot anu ochlin
chametz u matzah, chametz u matzah
Halailah hazeh, halailah hazeh kulo matzah
Halailah hazeh, halailah hazeh, kulo matzah

On all other nights we eat either leavened bread or *matzah*. On this night why only *matzah*?

(The adults answer):

On this night we eat only *matzah* to remind us that when our people were escaping to freedom they did not have time for the bread to rise.

(The children sing the Second Question):

שֶׁבְּכָל הַלֵּילוֹת אָנוּ אוֹכְלִין
שְׁאָר יְרָקוֹת, שְׁאָר יְרָקוֹת
הַלַיְלָה הַזֶּה, הַלַיְלָה הַזֶּה, מָרוֹר, מָרוֹר
הַלַיְלָה הַזֶּה, הַלַיְלָה הַזֶּה, מָרוֹר, מָרוֹר

Sheb'chol haleilot anu ochlin
she'ar yirakot, she'ar yirakot
Halailah hazeh, halailah hazeh,
halailah hazeh maror
Halailah hazeh, halailah hazeh,
halailah hazeh maror

On all other nights we eat many kinds of herbs. On this night why do we eat bitter herbs?

(The adults answer):

On this night we eat bitter herbs to remind us that the Egyptians made the lives of our ancestors bitter when they were slaves. Each year, as we sit together at the *Seder* table, we imagine that each of us went out of Egypt. The *Torah* teaches us: "You shall explain to your child on that day, it is because of what God did for me when I, myself, went out of Egypt."

(The children sing the Third Question):

שֶׁבְּכָל הַלֵּילוֹת אֵין אָנוּ מַטְבִּילִין
אֲפִילוּ פַּעַם אֶחָת, אֲפִילוּ פַּעַם אֶחָת
הַלַּיְלָה הַזֶּה, הַלַּיְלָה הַזֶּה, שְׁתֵּי פְּעָמִים
הַלַּיְלָה הַזֶּה, הַלַּיְלָה הַזֶּה, שְׁתֵּי פְּעָמִים

Sheb'chol halelilot ein anu matbilin
afilu pa-am echat, afilu pa-am echat
Halailah hazeh, halailah hazeh sh'tei pe'amim
Halailah hazeh, halailah hazeh sh'tei pe'amim

On all other nights we do not have to dip our herbs even once. On this night why do we dip them twice?

(The adults answer):

On this night we dip *karpas* in saltwater to remind us of the tears our people cried. We dip the *maror* in the *charoset* to remind us of the mortar the Jewish slaves used in our forced labor in Egypt. When we combine something bitter with something sweet, we remember that even when people are sad there is always hope for a happier time.

(The children sing the Fourth Question):

בְּכָל הַלֵּילוֹת אָנוּ אוֹכְלִין
בֵּין יוֹשְׁבִין וּבֵין מְסֻבִּין
הַלַּיְלָה הַזֶּה, הַלַּיְלָה הַזֶּה,
כֻּלָּנוּ מְסֻבִּין
הַלַּיְלָה הַזֶּה, הַלַּיְלָה הַזֶּה,
כֻּלָּנוּ מְסֻבִּין

Sheb'chol haleilot anu ochlin
bein yoshvin u'vein m'subin
Halailah hazeh, halailah hazeh,
kulanu m'subin
Halailah hazeh, halailah hazeh,
kulanu m'subin

On all other nights we eat our meals sitting any way we like. On this night, why do we lean and recline?

(The adults answer):

Long ago, free people could lean on a pillow during meals to relax and be comfortable while slaves served them food. On this night we recline to remind ourselves that once we were slaves but now we are free people, allowed to act as we desire. Tonight is a celebration of our liberties.

(All together):

At one time we were slaves of Pharaoh in Egypt, but God brought us out from there with a strong hand and an outstretched arm. If God had not rescued our forefathers, then we, our children, and our children's children might still be slaves in Egypt. Thus, even were we all wise, all people of understanding, and all well learned in the *Torah*, it would still be our duty to tell the story of the departure from Egypt. And the more we tell of the Exodus, the more are we to be praised.

(The leader says):

When we explain something, we want everyone to understand. This is especially true of the *Pesach* story. The *Torah* commands us four times that we must teach children about the Exodus from Egypt. These four commands suggest that there are four kinds of children, each of whom learns in a different way. Thus the *Torah* speaks about four sons: one who is wise, one who is contrary, one who is simple, and one who does not even know how to ask a question.

(Next participant):

The wise son asks: "What is the meaning of the laws which God has commanded to us? I want to know the meaning of all these rules." This child is proud to be a Jew and is interested in sharing experiences that are important to Jews. It is for this son that the story of Passover is told and the symbols explained.

(Next participant):

The contrary son asks: "What is the meaning of this service to you? Why do you bother with all these rules?" Saying "you," he excludes himself, and because he excludes himself from the group, he denies a basic principle. This child does not include himself in this question and acts like a stranger when attending a *Seder*. This son must be told that the Passover story is for him as much as for everyone else.

(Next participant):

The simple son asks: "What is this all about?" This child needs to understand basic facts. This son should be told that we do all these things because God freed us from slavery in Egypt.

(Next participant):
As for the son who does not even know how to ask a question, you must begin for him, as it is written in the *Torah*: "You shall tell your children on that day: 'This is done because of that which the Eternal did for me when I came forth out of Egypt.'" This child needs to learn about Judaism.

(The leader says):
Now we fulfill the *Pesach mitzvah* by telling the story of Passover.

(Next participant):
Jewish history began a long time ago. Our people have lived in many countries, celebrating life in Jewish ways. Throughout Jewish history, angry, frightened, and cruel people have wanted to hurt us, but we have maintained our patience, strength, pride, and hope.

(Next participant):
Abraham, the first Jew, came from a family of idol worshippers. He broke with their tradition and became a believer in the One God, Who promised him and his wife Sarah that their descendants would become a great people, as numerous as the stars in the sky.

(Next participant):
God led Abraham and Sarah to the land of Israel, which was then called Canaan. However, God warned that their descendants would be strangers in a strange land, enslaved for four hundred years. Indeed, this prophecy came true.

(All together):
Blessed be God, for God foretold the end of the bondage to Abraham at the Covenant of Sacrifices. For God said to Abraham: "Know you that your children will be strangers in a strange land. They will be enslaved there and will be oppressed for four hundred years. The nation who will oppress them shall however be judged. Afterward they will come forth with great wealth."

(The leader says):
Let's all raise our second cup of wine, though we will not be drinking it yet.

(EVERYONE RAISES THEIR CUP OF WINE and says together, without drinking):
This promise made to our forefathers also holds true for us. Many times they have risen against us to destroy us; in every generation they rise against us and seek our destruction. But time after time we survive as a people.

(The leader says):
Let's put down our cups and continue the story.

(EVERYONE PUTS DOWN THEIR CUP.)

(Next participant):
Abraham and Sarah had a son named Isaac. Isaac married Rebecca, and they had a son named Jacob. Jacob and his wife Rachel had a son named Joseph. Joseph came to live in Egypt. Because of his ability to interpret dreams, Joseph rose to power as an advisor to the Pharaoh.

(Next participant):
Joseph told the Pharaoh to build storehouses and fill them with grain. When years of famine struck, there was still food to eat in Egypt. The Pharaoh was so grateful that when Joseph's brothers came in search of food, he invited them and their families to settle in the area called Goshen. Thus, Jacob's household—known as Hebrews or Israelites—multiplied greatly and lived peacefully in Egypt.

(Next participant):

Many years later, a new Pharaoh came to rule Egypt. This Pharaoh did not remember Joseph and all he had done for the Egyptian people. He feared that the Israelites were becoming too numerous and too powerful and might side with the enemy if there should ever be a war. Thus, this Pharaoh made the Israelites into slaves.

(Next participant):

The Pharaoh forced the Israelites to do hard labor, building cities with bricks made of clay and straw. They knew neither peace nor rest, only misery and pain. As the *Torah* says: "They set taskmasters over the people of Israel to make them suffer with burden, and they built storage cities for Pharaoh."

(Next participant):

Hundreds of years later, fearing that an Israelite boy would soon be born who would free his slaves, a new Pharaoh ordered that every baby boy born to an Israelite woman be drowned in the Nile River. Two brave midwives did not do as the Pharaoh had ordered, instead allowing the infants to live.

(Next participant):

The two midwives had attended a couple named Amram and Yocheved. The parents hid their newborn son at home for three months. When his cries became too loud, Yocheved placed him in a basket on the river. Their daughter Miriam watched to see what would happen. When the Pharaoh's daughter came to bathe in the river, she discovered the basket.

(Next participant):

Feeling pity for the helpless child, the princess decided to keep him as her own and named him Moses, which means "drawn from water." Bravely, Miriam asked the princess if she needed a nurse to help her with the baby. The princess said yes, and so it happened that Yocheved was able to care for her own son and teach him about his heritage as a Jew.

(Next participant):

Moses would have lived at the Pharaoh's palace all his life, but he could not ignore the suffering of his people. One day, when he saw an Egyptian beating an Israelite slave, he was unable to control his anger, and he killed the Egyptian taskmaster. Knowing his life would be in danger once the news of his deed spread, Moses fled to the land of Midian, where he became a shepherd.

(Next participant):

While tending sheep on a mountain, Moses saw a bush that seemed to be on fire, but was not burning up. From the bush, he heard God's voice calling to him. God said, "I am the God of your ancestors. I have seen the suffering of the Israelites and have heard their cries. I am ready to take them out of Egypt and bring them to a new land, a land flowing with milk and honey."

(Next participant):

God told Moses to return to Egypt to bring the message of freedom to the Israelites and to warn the Pharaoh that God would bring plagues on the Egyptians if he did not let the slaves go free. With his older brother Aaron as spokesman, Moses went to the Pharaoh, Ramses II, asking him to free the Israelites.

(Next participant):

God brought signs and wonders, but the Pharaoh remained stubborn. He made the Israelites work even harder. Finally, God brought ten plagues on the Egyptians. Each one frightened the Pharaoh, and each time he promised to free the slaves. But the Pharaoh did not keep his word. It was only after the last plague, the death of the firstborn of the Egyptians, that the Pharaoh agreed to let the Israelites go.

(The leader says):

We have filled our cups to remember the joy in being able to leave Egypt. Yet our happiness is not complete, because the Egyptians, who are also God's children, suffered from the Pharaoh's evil ways. Therefore, we will spill a drop of wine from our cups with a finger as we say each plague.

(EVERYONE SPILLS A DROP OF WINE and says together):
Dahm (דָּם).

(Next participant):

Blood. There was blood in all the water of Egypt. The Egyptians could not bathe. They could not drink. They could not water their flowers or crops.

(EVERYONE SPILLS A DROP OF WINE and says together):
Ts'fardei-a (**צְפַרְדֵּעַ**).

(Next participant):
Frogs. There were frogs hopping and croaking throughout Egypt. No one could sleep or walk in peace. Everything seemed to be moving and people were dizzy.

(EVERYONE SPILLS A DROP OF WINE and says together):
Kineem (**כִּנִּים**).

(Next participant):
Lice. All the Egyptians had lice in their hair. They scratched their skin so hard that they were in pain all over their bodies.

(EVERYONE SPILLS A DROP OF WINE and
says together):
Arov (עָרוֹב).

(Next participant):
**Beasts. There were wild beasts in every corner
of Egypt. They galloped, slithered, growled,
roared, and clawed. Soon, there was no room
for people.**

(EVERYONE SPILLS A DROP OF WINE and
says together):
Dever (דֶּבֶר).

(Next participant):
**Cattle Diseases. There were cattle diseases
that could not be cured. Cattle became ill and
died, leaving the Egyptians hungry. Many of
the Egyptians also became ill.**

(EVERYONE SPILLS A DROP OF WINE and
says together):
Sh'chin (שְׁחִין).

(Next participant):
**Boils. There were boils on the skins of the
Egyptians. As the boils burst, they were in
constant pain. They could not even get
dressed without screaming in agony.**

(EVERYONE SPILLS A DROP OF WINE and
says together):
Barad (בָּרָד).

(Next participant):
**Hail. There was hail throughout Egypt. It
rained down as dangerous balls of ice. It
destroyed roofs and damaged crops.**

(EVERYONE SPILLS A DROP OF WINE and
says together):
Arbeh (אַרְבֶּה).

(Next participant):
**Locusts. There were locusts swarming over all
the trees and blades of grass in Egypt. The
buzzing was frightening. Vegetables and
fruits were gobbled up, and only dust
remained on the ground.**

(EVERYONE SPILLS A DROP OF WINE and
says together):
Choshech (חֹשֶׁךְ).

(Next participant):
**Darkness. There was darkness all day and all
night throughout Egypt. Every day was pitch
black. At night, not even moonlight or stars
appeared. People were always cold.**

(EVERYONE SPILLS A DROP OF WINE and
says together):
Makat B'chorot (מַכַּת בְּכוֹרוֹת).

(Next participant):
**Slaying of the Firstborn. The firstborn of
every Egyptian family died. The screams of
parents could be heard throughout the land.
The Israelites put lamb's blood on their
doorposts to mark their households as Jewish
so that God would pass over and not smite
their firstborn.**

(The leader says):
We continue with the story of Passover.

(Next participant):
**When the Israelites reached the Sea of Reeds,
God parted the waters to let them cross. But
Pharaoh regretted his decision and ordered
his army to bring them back. When his
soldiers began crossing the Sea of Reeds in
their chariots, God told Moses to lift his rod,
and the waters rushed back, drowning the
Egyptians and their horses.**

(All together):
**Thus, God fulfilled His promise and brought
us out of Egypt—with a strong hand and an
outstretched arm.**

(The leader says):

It is now time for us to raise the second cup of wine.

(EVERYONE RAISES THEIR CUP OF WINE.)

(All together):

After we were freed, a new and happy time began for our people. As they stood on the other side of the sea, they sang words we still sing today: "Who is like You, O God? You are the Eternal One, the One who saved us!"

(The leader says):

With this second cup of wine we remember the second promise God made to the Jewish people: "I will deliver you from their slavery."

(All together):

בָּרוּךְ אַתָּה אֲדֹנָי אֱלֹהֵינוּ מֶלֶךְ הָעוֹלָם, בּוֹרֵא פְּרִי הַגָּפֶן.

Baruch atah Adonai Ellohaynu mellach ha'olam bowray paree hagafen.

Blessed art Thou, Eternal our God, King of the Universe, Creator of the fruit of the vine.

(The leader says):
Let's all drink our second cup of wine.

(EVERYONE DRINKS THE SECOND CUP OF WINE.)

(The leader says):
Let's all refill our cups so we can raise them shortly after we sing *"Dayenu."*

(EVERYONE FILLS THEIR CUP.)

(The leader says):
***Pesach* is a time to thank God for making our lives and our world better. The song *"Dayenu"* teaches us to switch from the mentality of always wanting more to being grateful for what we have. *Dayenu* (דַּיֵּנוּ) means "that alone would have been enough." Let us hear what the verses of the song *"Dayenu"* communicate.**

41

(Next participant):

If God had only brought us out of Egypt, that alone would have been enough.

(All together):
Dayenu (דַּיֵּינוּ).

(Next participant):

If God had only given us the Sabbath, that alone would have been enough.

(All together):
Dayenu.

(Next participant):

If God had only given us the *Torah*, that alone would have been enough.

(All together):

Dayenu.* For all of these—alone and together—we say: *Dayenu.

(Everyone sings together):

אִלוּ הוֹצִיא הוֹצִיאָנוּ
הוֹצִיאָנוּ מִמִּצְרַיִם
מִמִּצְרַיִם הוֹצִיאָנוּ
דַּיֵּנוּ

Ilu hotzi hotzianu
Hotzianu mimitzrayim
Mimitzrayim hotzianu
Dayenu

דַּי דַּיֵּנוּ, דַּי דַּיֵּנוּ
דַּי דַּיֵּנוּ, דַּיֵּנוּ, דַּיֵּנוּ
דַּי דַּיֵּנוּ, דַּי דַּיֵּנוּ
דַּי דַּיֵּנוּ, דַּיֵּנוּ, דַּיֵּנוּ

Da dayenu, da dayenu
Da dayenu, dayenu, dayenu
Da dayenu, da dayenu
Da dayenu, dayenu, dayenu

אִלוּ נָתַן נָתַן לָנוּ
נָתַן לָנוּ אֶת הַשַּׁבָּת
אֶת הַשַּׁבָּת, אֶת הַשַּׁבָּת
דַּיֵּנוּ

Ilu natan natan lanu
Natan lanu et hashabbat
Et hashabbat, Et hashabbat
Dayenu

43

דַי דַיֵּינוּ, דַי דַיֵּינוּ
דַי דַיֵּינוּ, דַיֵּינוּ, דַיֵּינוּ
דַי דַיֵּינוּ, דַי דַיֵּינוּ
דַי דַיֵּינוּ, דַיֵּינוּ, דַיֵּינוּ

Da dayenu, da dayenu
Da dayenu, dayenu, dayenu
Da dayenu, da dayenu
Da dayenu, dayenu, dayenu

אִלּוּ נָתַן נָתַן לָנוּ
נָתַן לָנוּ אֶת הַתּוֹרָה
אֶת הַתּוֹרָה, תּוֹרָה טוֹבָה
דַיֵּינוּ

Ilu natan natan lanu
Natan lanu et hatorah
Et hatorah, Torah tova
Dayenu

דַי דַיֵּינוּ, דַי דַיֵּינוּ
דַי דַיֵּינוּ, דַיֵּינוּ, דַיֵּינוּ
דַי דַיֵּינוּ, דַי דַיֵּינוּ
דַי דַיֵּינוּ, דַיֵּינוּ, דַיֵּינוּ

Da dayenu, da dayenu
Da dayenu, dayenu, dayenu
Da dayenu, da dayenu
Da dayenu, dayenu, dayenu

(The leader says):

Let's all raise our cups of wine, though we will not be drinking yet.

(EVERYONE RAISES THEIR CUP OF WINE
and says together, without drinking):

בְּכָל דּוֹר וָדוֹר חַיָּב אָדָם לִרְאוֹת אֶת עַצְמוֹ כְּאִלוּ הוּא יָצָא מִמִּצְרַיִם.

B'chol dor vador chayav adam lirot et atzmo k'ilu hu yatza mi'Mitzrayim.

In each generation, everyone must think of himself or herself as having personally left Egypt.

We traditionally give thanks, sing praises, and offer blessings to the Holy One, Who did these miracles for our ancestors and for us. He brought us from slavery to freedom, from sadness to joy, and from darkness to light.

(The leader says):

Let's set down our cups and continue.

(EVERYONE PUTS DOWN THEIR CUP.)

(Next participant):
We should be grateful to God for the doubled and redoubled goodness that He has bestowed upon us. For He has brought us out of Egypt, and carried out judgments against the Egyptians and their idols, and smote their firstborn, and gave us their wealth, and split the sea for us, and took us through it on dry land, and drowned our enemies in it.

(Next participant):
And God's goodness didn't stop there. We should continue to be thankful for the other things He did and continues to do. He supplied our needs in the desert for forty years, and gave us *Shabbat*, and brought us before Mount Sinai, and gave us the Ten Commandments, and brought us into the land of Israel so we could build the Temple in Jerusalem.

(The leader says):
It is now time to wash our hands again for the meal. Since we've already washed the traditional way, this time we will use moist towels. We will also say a blessing this time.

(PRE-MOISTENED HAND TOWELS ARE DISTRIBUTED. IF DESIRED, WARM IN THE MICROWAVE BEFOREHAND.)

(EVERYONE WASHES THEIR HANDS FOR
THE MEAL and says together):

בָּרוּךְ אַתָּה אֲדֹנָי אֱלֹהֵינוּ מֶלֶךְ הָעוֹלָם, אֲשֶׁר קִדְּשָׁנוּ
בְּמִצְוֹתָיו וְצִוָּנוּ עַל נְטִילַת יָדָיִם.

*Baruch atah Adonai Ellohaynu mellach
ha'olam asher kid'shanu b'mitzvolav v'tzivanu
al n'tilat yadayim.*

Blessed are Thou, Eternal our God, King of
the Universe, Who makes us holy by Your
mitzvot and commands us to wash our hands.

(THE TOWELS ARE COLLECTED AND
REMOVED FROM THE TABLE.)

(The leader says):
We have fulfilled the *mitzvah* of the telling of
the Passover Story, and we've learned the
meaning of our *Pesach* foods. Now we are
ready to eat the rest of them, starting with the
matzah to remind
us of our hurried
exodus from Egypt.
Please take a piece
of *matzah* and we'll
recite the blessing
together.

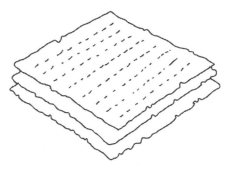

(EVERYONE TAKES A PIECE OF *MATZAH*
and says together):

בָּרוּךְ אַתָּה אֲדֹנָי אֱלֹהֵינוּ מֶלֶךְ הָעוֹלָם, הַמּוֹצִיא לֶחֶם
מִן הָאָרֶץ.

Baruch atah Adonai Ellohaynu mellach ha'olam ha'motzi lechem min ha'aretz.

Blessed art Thou, Eternal our God, King of the Universe, Who brings forth bread from the earth.

בָּרוּךְ אַתָּה אֲדֹנָי אֱלֹהֵינוּ מֶלֶךְ הָעוֹלָם, אֲשֶׁר קִדְּשָׁנוּ
בְּמִצְוֹתָיו וְצִוָּנוּ עַל אֲכִילַת מַצָּה.

Baruch atah Adonai Ellohaynu mellach ha'olam ashare kid'shanu b'mitzvotav v'tzivanu al achilat matzah.

Blessed art Thou, Eternal our God, King of the Universe, Who made us holy with His commandments, and commands us to eat *matzah*.

(The leader says):
Let's all enjoy our *matzah* while reclining to celebrate our freedom.

(EVERYONE EATS THE *MATZAH* WHILE RECLINING.)

(The leader says):

It is now time to take a piece of bitter herb and dip it in the sweet *charoset*. Before eating it, we'll recite the blessing together.

(EVERYONE TAKES A PIECE OF BITTER HERB AND DIPS IT IN THE *CHAROSET.*)

(The leader says):

We dip the *maror* into *charoset* to recall that our ancestors were able to withstand the bitterness of slavery because it was sweetened by the hope of freedom.

(All together):

בָּרוּךְ אַתָּה אֲדֹנָי אֱלֹהֵינוּ מֶלֶךְ הָעוֹלָם, אֲשֶׁר קִדְּשָׁנוּ בְּמִצְוֹתָיו וְצִוָּנוּ עַל אֲכִילַת מָרוֹר.

Baruch atah Adonai Ellohaynu mellach ha'olam ashare kid'shanu b'mitzvotav v'tzivanu al achilat maror.

Blessed art Thou, Eternal our God, King of the Universe, Who made us holy with His commandments, and commanded us concerning the eating of bitter herbs.

(The leader says):
Let's all eat our sweetened bitter herbs while reclining to celebrate our freedom.

(EVERYONE EATS THE BITTER HERB WHILE RECLINING.)

(The leader says):
It is now time to make a sandwich using two pieces of *matzah*, some bitter herb, and the sweet *charoset*. We'll recite a few lines before eating it.

(EVERYONE MAKES A SANDWICH OF *MATZAH*, BITTER HERB AND *CHAROSET*.)

(The leader says):
We remember that even though we are free, there are still people who are not yet free.

(All together):
Hillel, a famous rabbi in the days of the Holy Temple, taught us to eat a sandwich of *matzah*, bitter herb and *charoset*. By doing so, we put together the *matzah* of freedom and the *maror* and *charoset* of slavery. Where people are not free, there will always be the hope of freedom.

(The leader says):
Let's all eat our sandwiches while reclining to celebrate our freedom.

(EVERYONE EATS THEIR SANDWICH WHILE RECLINING.)

(Next participant):
There is an old *Sephardic* tradition of having the firstborn *Seder* participants share a roasted egg as a sign of gratitude to God for sparing the Jewish firstborn during the tenth plague.

(Next participant):
Today we serve hard-boiled eggs at the beginning of the meal, as a symbol of spring and renewal. They also remind us of the brave Jewish midwives who refused to carry out Pharaoh's order to kill the male babies, and thus assured Jewish survival.

(The leader says):
Let's all eat our hard-boiled eggs and then the rest of our festival meal!

(EVERYONE EATS THEIR HARD-BOILED EGG.)

The Festival Meal Is Served!

**Do not serve dessert.
During the meal, the children steal
the *afikoman* and hide it.**

(After the meal, the leader says):
Where is the *afikoman*? We cannot finish our meal without the *afikoman*! It is our traditional dessert!

(The children say):
We've hidden the *afikoman*. You must bargain with us to get it back.

(THE CHILDREN BARGAIN WITH THEIR ELDERS FOR THE RETURN OF THE *AFIKOMAN*. WHEN AN AGREEMENT IS REACHED, THE *MATZAH* IS RETURNED.)

(The leader says):
We will each take part of the *afikoman* and enjoy our share while reclining to celebrate our freedom.

(THE LEADER BREAKS UP THE *AFIKOMAN*. AFTER IT IS DISTRIBUTED, EVERYONE EATS THEIR SHARE WHILE RECLINING.)

(Next participant):
The *afikoman* is shared just as the *Pesach* offering was shared in the days of the Temple, to show that we are all friends with one another. No special blessing is said, because the dessert is part of the meal.

(The leader says):

It is now time to conclude our *Seder*. If your cup isn't already full, please fill it for the third cup of wine.

(EVERYONE FILLS THEIR CUP FOR THE THIRD CUP OF WINE.)

(The leader says):

Now is the time to give thanks to God for what we have eaten. We call this the *Hallel*.

(All together):

בָּרוּךְ אַתָּה אֲדֹנָי הַזָּן אֶת הַכֹּל.

Baruch atah Adonai hazan et-hakol.

Blessed art Thou, Eternal our God, in Whose world there is food for all life.

May the Holy One make peace for us, for Israel, and for all the world.

Praise the Eternal, all ye nations; praise Him, all ye people! For His kindness overwhelms us, and the truth of the Eternal is forever. Hallelujah!

(The leader says):
It is now time to raise our third cup of wine.

(EVERYONE RAISES THE THIRD CUP OF
WINE, and the leader says):
**With this third cup of wine we remember the
third promise God made to the Jewish people:
"I will redeem you with an outstretched arm."**

(All together):
בָּרוּךְ אַתָּה אֲדֹנָי אֱלֹהֵינוּ מֶלֶךְ הָעוֹלָם, בּוֹרֵא פְּרִי
הַגָּפֶן.

*Baruch   atah   Adonai   Ellohaynu   mellach
ha'olam bowray paree hagafen.*

**Blessed art Thou, Eternal our God, King of
the Universe, Creator of the fruit of the vine.**

(The leader says):
Let's all drink our third cup of wine, then fill our cups for the fourth and final cup. I shall fill a special cup for Elijah the Prophet.

(EVERYONE DRINKS THE THIRD CUP OF WINE AND THEN REFILLS THEIR CUP. THE LEADER FILLS THE CUP FOR ELIJAH THE PROPHET.)

(The leader says):
This is the Watchnight of the Eternal.

(Next participant):
There is an extra cup of wine on our *Seder* table: the Cup of Elijah. When the Prophet Elijah comes, he will announce a time when all the people in the world will be free. Each and every one of us has a responsibility to help bring freedom to all and make the prophet's words come true.

(Next participant):
Historically, *Pesach* Eve was also called the "Night of Watching." The door was left open as if participants were ready to leave at a moment's notice.

(Next participant):
As it is sometimes dangerous to keep doors open, the practice changed. Now we open the door for just a few minutes. This custom became associated with Elijah, who, legend says, visits the *Seder* each year.

(The leader says):
It is traditional for the children to open the door and welcome Elijah into our home. Let's all rise and wait while the children go open the door.

(EVERYONE RISES. THE ADULTS WAIT WHILE THE CHILDREN OPEN THE DOOR AND RETURN TO THE TABLE. EVERYONE REMAINS STANDING.)

(Next participant):
We've opened a door to the outside and hope that Elijah will come now. May these words of the *Torah* come true tonight: "Behold, I will send you Elijah the Prophet, who will turn the hearts of the parents to the children and the hearts of the children to the parents before the coming of the great and mighty Day of God!"

(Next participant):

This cup is for *Eliyahu Hanavi* (אֵלִיָּהוּ הַנָּבִיא),
Elijah the Prophet. We open our door to greet
our honored guest and invite him to join our
Seder. We pray that he will return to us,
bringing a time of peace and freedom.

(EVERYONE sings):

אֵלִיָּהוּ הַנָּבִיא, אֵלִיָּהוּ הַתִּשְׁבִּי
אֵלִיָּהוּ, אֵלִיָּהוּ, אֵלִיָּהוּ הַגִּלְעָדִי

Eliyahu Hanavi, Eliyahu Ha'tishbi
Eliyahu, Eliyahu, Eliyahu Ha'giladi.

(All together):

May Elijah the Prophet come to us quickly
and in our day, bringing the time of the
Messiah.

(The leader says):

Children, please close the door now. The rest
of us will take our seats and wait for you to
return.

(THE CHILDREN CLOSE THE DOOR AND
RETURN TO THE TABLE. ALL ARE
SEATED.)

(The leader says):
We will now conclude our *Seder*.

(All together):
This is the Passover Festival!

(Next participant):
The table was set and all arranged on Passover. To Abraham, God was revealed on Passover. The mighty power of God was displayed on Passover.

(All together):
This is the Passover Festival!

(Next participant):
Cakes of unleavened bread were prepared for visitors on Passover. Lot baked unleavened bread on Passover. The cities of Sodom and Gomorrah were consumed by fire on Passover.

(All together):
This is the Passover Festival!

(Next participant):
Lamb shanks were roasted for all to remember the sacrifice on Passover. God permitted no destroyer to enter Israel's doors on Passover. God smote the firstborn on the Watchnight of Passover.

(All together):
This is the Passover Festival!

(Next participant):
Four cups of wine were consumed on Passover. The walls of Jericho fell on Passover. Midian was destroyed on Passover.

(All together):
This is the Passover Festival!

Next participant):
Blessings and songs of praise were sung on Passover. Jacob wrestled with an angel and won on Passover. The hand wrote on the wall in Babylon on Passover.

(All together):
This is the Passover Festival!

(Next participant):
The blessings of freedom were remembered on Passover. Queen Esther assembled the community to fast three days at Passover. Haman was hanged on the gallows on Passover.

(All together):
This is the Passover Festival!

(The leader says):
It is now time to raise our fourth cup of wine. We will recite a few lines before saying the blessing and drinking it.

(EVERYONE RAISES THEIR CUP OF WINE and says):
God promised Abraham that after four hundred years of servitude, his descendants would leave the land of their bondage and witness the judgment of their oppressors. It is this promise that sustains the Jewish people in each generation, as enemies arise to destroy us. Thus, we are able to say, *Am Yisrael Chai* (עַם יִשְׂרָאֵל חַי), the Jewish people live.

61

(The leader says):

Our *Seder* is almost over. We lift our cups for the last time. With this fourth cup of wine we remember the fourth promise to the Jewish people: "And I will take you to be my people."

(All together):

בָּרוּךְ אַתָּה אֲדֹנָי אֱלֹהֵינוּ מֶלֶךְ הָעוֹלָם, בּוֹרֵא פְּרִי הַגָּפֶן.

Baruch atah Adonai Ellohaynu mellach ha'olam bowray paree hagafen.

Blessed art Thou, Eternal our God, King of the Universe, Creator of the fruit of the vine.

(The leader says):

Let's now drink our fourth cup of wine.

(EVERYONE DRINKS THE FOURTH CUP OF WINE.)

(Next participant):
The Jewish people are not the only group to have been made slaves and oppressed. Our duty to remember our own hardships should also include the recognition of the suffering of other nations, races, and ethnicities. One group to have suffered in America was the African slaves who worked the fields of Southern plantations. They remembered our suffering to inspire their own pursuit of freedom. We should not forget theirs.

(The leader says):
"Go Down Moses" is an African-American spiritual that was sung throughout the South by slaves while they worked. It was also sung by abolitionists to signal escape or rebellion. Let us acknowledge our shared struggle by singing it now.

(Everyone sings together):
When Israel was in Egypt land
Let my people go!
Oppressed so hard they could not stand
Let my people go!

Go down, Moses
Way down in Egypt land
Tell 'ol Pharaoh
Let my people go!

63

"Thou saith the Lord," bold Moses said
Let my people go!
"If not, I'll smite your firstborn dead"
Let my people go!

Go down, Moses
Way down in Egypt land
Tell 'ol Pharaoh
Let my people go!

The Lord told Moses what to do
Let my people go!
To lead the children of Israel through
Let my people go!

Go down, Moses
Way down in Egypt land
Tell 'ol Pharaoh
Let my people go!

When they had reached the other shore
Let my people go!
They sang a song of triumph o'er
Let my people go!

Go down, Moses
Way down in Egypt land
Tell 'ol Pharaoh
Let my people go!

(Next participant):

The *Talmud* says that when we tell the story of
Pesach, we should begin with despair and end
with joy. Tonight we did this in two ways.
First, we began by telling how our ancestors
were idol worshippers and came to worship
only God and follow his Commandments.
Second, we related how our people were
slaves in Egypt, and how God brought them
to freedom.

(Next participant):

According to *Chasidic* teaching, the real
slavery in Egypt was that the Israelites had
learned to endure it. We must remember this
and vigorously expand our own freedoms.
Even we, who live in relative freedom today,
should not forget how easily these freedoms
can be lost and how dangerous the limits to
our freedom can be.

(Next participant):

In every generation, each Jew should regard
himself as though he too were brought out of
Egypt. It was not only in Egypt, but in many
other lands, that we have cried under the
burden of affliction and suffered as victims of
malice, ignorance, and racism.

(Next participant):

This very night, which we, a happy generation, celebrate so safely and joyfully in our homes, was often a night of anxiety and suffering for our people in former times. Cruel mobs were ready to rush upon them and to destroy their homes and the fruit of their labors. But they clung to their faith in the ultimate triumph of right and of freedom.

(Next participant):

Our ancestors marched from one Egypt to another—driven in haste, with their bundles on their shoulders and God in their hearts. Because God, "the Guardian of Israel," revealed Himself on the Watchnight in Egypt and in all dark periods of our past, we keep this night as a watchnight for all the children of Israel.

(Next participant):

While enjoying the liberty of this land, let us strive to keep secure our spiritual freedom. Through this freedom, we may also carry out the Jewish people's historic task of being the messenger of religious tolerance and of justice unto all mankind.

(All together):

Blessed art Thou, Eternal our God, King of the Universe, Creator of innumerable living beings. We thank Thee for all the means that Thou hast created to sustain all. Blessed be the Eternal.

(The leader says):

Our *Seder* now concludes, and is complete according to our laws and traditions. Just as we were fortunate to perform it this evening, so may we be able to do so again next year. May there be freedom and peace for us! For everyone!

(All together):

NEXT YEAR IN JERUSALEM!

After the *Seder*, please sign one of these pages to add to the record of our yearly celebrations!

SIGNATURE

DATE

MESSAGE OR MEMORY:

SIGNATURE

DATE

MESSAGE OR MEMORY:

After the *Seder*, please sign one of these pages to add to the record of our yearly celebrations!

SIGNATURE

DATE

MESSAGE OR MEMORY:

SIGNATURE

DATE

MESSAGE OR MEMORY:

After the *Seder*, please sign one of these pages to add to the record of our yearly celebrations!

SIGNATURE

DATE

MESSAGE OR MEMORY:

SIGNATURE

DATE

MESSAGE OR MEMORY:

After the *Seder*, please sign one of these pages to add to the record of our yearly celebrations!

SIGNATURE

DATE

MESSAGE OR MEMORY:

SIGNATURE

DATE

MESSAGE OR MEMORY:

After the *Seder*, please sign one of these pages to add to the record of our yearly celebrations!

SIGNATURE

DATE

MESSAGE OR MEMORY:

SIGNATURE

DATE

MESSAGE OR MEMORY:

After the *Seder*, please sign one of these pages to add to the record of our yearly celebrations!

SIGNATURE

DATE

MESSAGE OR MEMORY:

SIGNATURE

DATE

MESSAGE OR MEMORY:

After the *Seder*, please sign one of these pages to add to the record of our yearly celebrations!

SIGNATURE

DATE

MESSAGE OR MEMORY:

SIGNATURE

DATE

MESSAGE OR MEMORY:

After the *Seder*, please sign one of these pages to add to the record of our yearly celebrations!

SIGNATURE

DATE

MESSAGE OR MEMORY:

SIGNATURE

DATE

MESSAGE OR MEMORY:

After the *Seder*, please sign one of these pages to add to the record of our yearly celebrations!

SIGNATURE

DATE

MESSAGE OR MEMORY:

SIGNATURE

DATE

MESSAGE OR MEMORY:

After the *Seder*, please sign one of these pages to add to the record of our yearly celebrations!

SIGNATURE

DATE

MESSAGE OR MEMORY:

SIGNATURE

DATE

MESSAGE OR MEMORY:

After the *Seder*, please sign one of these pages to add to the record of our yearly celebrations!

SIGNATURE

DATE

MESSAGE OR MEMORY:

SIGNATURE

DATE

MESSAGE OR MEMORY:

After the *Seder*, please sign one of these pages to add to the record of our yearly celebrations!

SIGNATURE

DATE

MESSAGE OR MEMORY:

SIGNATURE

DATE

MESSAGE OR MEMORY:

After the *Seder*, please sign one of these pages to add to the record of our yearly celebrations!

SIGNATURE

DATE

MESSAGE OR MEMORY:

SIGNATURE

DATE

MESSAGE OR MEMORY:

After the *Seder*, please sign one of these pages to add to the record of our yearly celebrations!

SIGNATURE

DATE

MESSAGE OR MEMORY:

SIGNATURE

DATE

MESSAGE OR MEMORY:

After the *Seder*, please sign one of these pages to add to the record of our yearly celebrations!

SIGNATURE

DATE

MESSAGE OR MEMORY:

SIGNATURE

DATE

MESSAGE OR MEMORY:

After the *Seder*, please sign one of these pages to add to the record of our yearly celebrations!

SIGNATURE

DATE

MESSAGE OR MEMORY:

SIGNATURE

DATE

MESSAGE OR MEMORY:

After the *Seder*, please sign one of these pages to add to the record of our yearly celebrations!

SIGNATURE

DATE

MESSAGE OR MEMORY:

SIGNATURE

DATE

MESSAGE OR MEMORY:

After the *Seder*, please sign one of these pages to add to the record of our yearly celebrations!

SIGNATURE

DATE

MESSAGE OR MEMORY:

SIGNATURE

DATE

MESSAGE OR MEMORY:

After the *Seder*, please sign one of these pages to add to the record of our yearly celebrations!

SIGNATURE

DATE

MESSAGE OR MEMORY:

SIGNATURE

DATE

MESSAGE OR MEMORY:

After the *Seder*, please sign one of these pages to add to the record of our yearly celebrations!

SIGNATURE

DATE

MESSAGE OR MEMORY:

SIGNATURE

DATE

MESSAGE OR MEMORY:

After the *Seder*, please sign one of these pages to add to the record of our yearly celebrations!

SIGNATURE

DATE

MESSAGE OR MEMORY:

SIGNATURE

DATE

MESSAGE OR MEMORY:

After the *Seder*, please sign one of these pages to add to the record of our yearly celebrations!

SIGNATURE

DATE

MESSAGE OR MEMORY:

SIGNATURE

DATE

MESSAGE OR MEMORY:

After the *Seder*, please sign one of these pages to add to the record of our yearly celebrations!

SIGNATURE

DATE

MESSAGE OR MEMORY:

SIGNATURE

DATE

MESSAGE OR MEMORY: